W9-BXS-611

1/06

NATURE'S PREDATORS

Coyotes

Other titles in the Nature's Predators series include:

Coyotes

Teresa L. Hyman

**KIDHAVEN
PRESS**™

THOMSON
™
GALE

San Diego • Detroit • New York • San Francisco • Cleveland
New Haven, Conn. • Waterville, Maine • London • Munich

LIBRARY OF CONGRESS CATALOGING-IN-PUBLICATION DATA

Hyman, Teresa L.
  Coyotes / by Teresa L. Hyman
    p. cm. — (Nature's Predators)
Summary: Discusses coyotes including habitat, physical characteristics, hunting
practices, and threats faced by humans.
Includes bibliographical references and index.
  ISBN 0-7377-1886-2 (hardback : alk. paper)
  1. Coyote—Juvenile literature. [1. Coyote.] I. Title. II. Series.
  QL737.C22H95 2004
  599.77'25—dc21

                    2003007298

CONTENTS

CHAPTER ONE

A Most Perfect Predator

Two fuzzy, doglike coyotes trot along under the Nevada moon. Noses to the ground, they look like German shepherds, only lighter and narrower. They sniff the ground as they make zigzag patterns in the scarce grass. They are searching for a meal.

One of the pair stops abruptly, causing puffs of dusty clouds to rise in the darkening sky. It begins to dig at the earth with its quick, broad paws. The other coyote quickly scurries off to the right, its nose still close to the desert floor. Suddenly, a small rabbit pops out of an almost perfectly camouflaged hole. The coyote catches the rabbit in its narrow, powerful jaws.

Its partner stops digging at the other end of the rabbit hole. Once again, their hunt has been successful.

Once the meal is finished, the pair moves on. Perhaps, on the next hunt, they will stumble upon a dead deer and have a true feast. The coyotes—two of nature's most perfect **predators**—trot across the plain searching for their next meal.

Barking Dog

The coyote gets its name from the Aztec word *coyotl* which means "barking dog." The name refers to the *yip-yip-haw-oooo* sound the animal makes and to its

Range of the Coyote

ALASKA

CANADA

Pacific Ocean

UNITED STATES

Atlantic Ocean

CENTRAL AMERICA

☐ Coyote Range

physical likeness to dogs. There are millions of coyotes living in North America. They are found as far north as Canada and Alaska and as far south as Central America. Although most coyotes are found in open, prairie areas, they can survive almost anywhere, including forests, deserts, mountains, and even cities.

There are about nineteen different kinds, or **subspecies**, of coyotes. The differences between them are so small that scientists often have trouble telling one subspecies from another. Their head size, fur color, and weight often vary. Coyotes can come in many different colors, from reddish gray or gray-black to creamy white and brown. Desert coyotes can weigh up to twenty pounds, while those living in mountain regions can weigh up to forty pounds.

The Pack

Coyotes may live and hunt alone, in pairs, or in a pack. A coyote pack is usually made up of a coyote and its mate—called the **alpha** pair—and their young offspring. Sometimes, however, a pack can be made up of the alpha pair and several related coyotes like aunts, brothers, or sisters. The size of a pack depends on the size of the territory and the amount and kinds of food available. In places where there are large prey such as deer and elk, more coyotes are required to bring down the animals, and pack numbers tend to be larger. In areas such as the desert, it is possible to have only the alpha pair and no other coyotes. On average, there could be four to fifteen coyotes in a pack.

The alpha male and alpha female are the only coyotes within the pack that are allowed to mate. The other coyotes, called betas or associates, help the alpha pair raise and protect the pups. These associates eventually venture off to start families and territories of their own. Some may leave the pack and hunt alone for a few seasons only to return months, even a year or two, later.

A coyote establishes its own territory—usually an area of about thirty square miles—and sticks to that territory when hunting and raising its family. It marks its territory by urinating at certain spots and by leaving its **scat**, or droppings, on trails where other coyotes will see or smell it. It protects its territory by fighting off coyotes that try to take over. The coyote usually travels within its boundaries to find the food it needs. However, in times when food is scarce, the coyote may move beyond its own territory to hunt or **scavenge**.

Coyotes are **omnivores**, meaning they eat other animals as well as vegetables and fruits. Those living in forests may hunt wild birds and squirrels. Coyotes in desert areas eat insects, small lizards, and mice. Those that live in or near cities can survive by eating rats or rotting food found in garbage cans. All coyotes will feed on dead animals, or **carrion**, such as deer killed by hunters or possums found along highways. A coyote also eats eggs, fish, snakes, grass, vegetables, and fruits.

A coyote crosses a creek. Coyotes usually hunt and raise families within their own territories.

Because of its varied diet and **habitat** the coyote must **adapt**, to, or fit into, almost any environment. Its body is designed to help it do just that.

Built for Success

Measuring between fifteen and twenty inches high at the shoulders and weighing fifteen to forty-five pounds, coyotes are agile and light on their feet. Their long, thin legs are very muscular, making it easy for them to run long distances and jump effortlessly. They can run as fast as twenty miles per hour. Some have even been recorded at forty miles

A coyote stands over a dead bird. Coyotes hunt a variety of small animals for food.

A coyote pounces on a mouse. Coyotes have powerful legs that allow them to quickly jump very high.

per hour when running short sprints during a hunt. Their powerful legs allow them to crunch through packed snow or ice to find rodents. Coyotes can jump up to ten feet high in order to catch a fleeing rabbit or rodent such as a vole.

Coyotes' paws are narrow and made for digging, pulling, and scratching. With their strong feet, they dig dens for themselves and their pups. They also dig into holes made by rabbits, mice, and other small animals when searching for a meal. Their sharp claws allow them to climb steep, rocky ledges and provide them with traction when walking over shifting desert sand or slick ice.

A coyote's long, narrow jaws hold special teeth that clamp down on, shred, or crush its meal. Four sharp fangs—two in the top jaw and two in the bottom—at the front of a coyote's mouth grab its food. The fangs sink into the flesh of an animal, allowing the coyote to hang on to even the squirmiest lizard, rabbit, or bird. The fangs also help it hold on to hard objects such as apples and watermelons or fruits with tough skins such as oranges. Behind the fangs are the sectoral teeth, or premolars. These teeth act as scissors. They shred the coyote's meal into pieces that are easier to swallow. The molars at the back of its mouth crush the coyote's food. This allows the coyote to get the nutrients found in the marrow of its prey's bones. The coyote's front teeth, the incisors, are used to scrape the last pieces of meat and gristle from bones.

With legs made for strength, paws for digging, and sharp claws and teeth for hunting prey, coyotes are impressive creatures. But, add their keen senses, and the coyote becomes one of nature's most successful predators.

Powerful Senses

Coyotes have a keen sense of smell, excellent hearing, and great eyesight. These senses help coyotes stay near the top of the **food chain** in their habitats. A coyote's mouth and nose are filled with millions

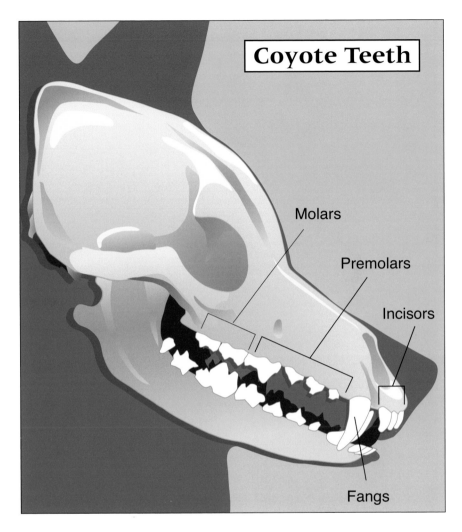

Coyote Teeth

Molars

Premolars

Incisors

Fangs

of tiny cells that can pick up smells up to two miles away. The coyote uses its sense of smell to track prey, to follow the smell of nearby dead animals or open trash cans, or to identify other coyotes and their territories.

Coyotes use their excellent hearing to catch their prey and to locate each other. Coyotes can hear field mice scurrying beneath up to six inches of snow and

Coyotes have excellent hearing. They can move their ears back and forth to zoom in on a sound.

can even hear the steps of faraway lizards. They move their large ears back and forth to zoom in on a sound and locate its source. In this way, they can identify the cries of other members of their family or note the howls of unfamiliar coyotes.

Coyotes also have great eyesight. They use their eyes to spot holes in fences, locate their prey, and identify weaknesses such as a broken wing or a limp. By noticing a hole in a farmer's fence, a coyote can sneak into a chicken coop and steal eggs. Once its sharp eyes have detected the broken wing of a goose, the coyote knows which goose in a flock is the easiest to kill. Noticing small details such as these helps the coyote plan its attack.

Even though a coyote is swift, agile, and has great senses of hearing and smell, it can still be challenging for it to find food. This is when the animal's craftiness comes into play.

CHAPTER TWO

Scavenging and Hunting

It can be difficult for the coyote to find enough food. It may try ten times to catch and eat prey but only succeed a few of those times. The catch may also be disappointing. A five-ounce field mouse or a small bird or ground squirrel alone will not fill the hungry coyote's belly. A medium-sized coyote needs from one and a half to four pounds of meat a day to survive. So, a coyote may have to kill several small animals over the course of a day to get the meat it needs.

Coyotes have many ways of finding food. In places where the weather is harsh or food is scarce, coyotes scavenge for food. They feed on dead animals, search through garbage, and eat almost anything they find in

A coyote munches on a bird. Coyotes need to eat several pounds of meat each day to survive.

order to survive. In addition to scavenging, coyotes are also organized hunters.

Scavenging

The coyote will eat almost anything. Although it prefers fresh meat, a coyote will also eat carrion when no fresh meat can be found. It feeds on animals or animal parts that human hunters leave behind or dead animals that have been hit by cars.

The coyote uses its acute sense of smell to locate and follow the scent of a dead animal. It hunches its back, drops its nose to the ground, and searches for the smell of dead flesh. Once the coyote has located the scent, it follows it, keeping its nose to the ground and its ears up, listening for danger. When the coyote finds the carcass, it may howl to communicate the location of the animal's body to its mate or others within the pack.

For coyotes living near people, scavenging is their most successful way of finding food. These coyotes sniff out garbage cans behind houses, dumpsters near buildings, city sewers, and landfills. They use their sharp claws and teeth to tear plastic garbage bags and their strong legs and jaws to knock away trash can lids. The coyotes then rummage through the garbage and make their meals from the food humans have discarded. Sometimes the coyotes eat old bits of cloth or leather, even shoestrings, to relieve their hunger. While searching for discarded food, coyotes encounter and prey upon rats, mice, and other rodents that also live on human trash.

A coyote gnaws on a carcass. Although coyotes prefer fresh meat, they will feed on dead animals.

While scavenging for food, a coyote makes meals out of vegetables and fruits such as watermelons and berries. It will steal fresh vegetables from the back of a grocery truck or use its long snout and sharp front teeth to grasp a tomato through a garden fence. A coyote also snacks on berries growing on bushes in the forest or on the side of a highway. In cities, coyotes steal dog food left outside for family pets.

The Tricky Coyote

Though scavenging keeps a coyote from starving, the real business of staying alive is found in the hunt. A coyote may hunt alone, with other coyotes, or

A coyote spots a potential meal. Coyotes may hunt alone or with other coyotes.

---

even use other kinds of animals to help it find its prey.

When hunting alone, a coyote will eat anything it comes across. Birds, lizards, small rodents, and even pets like cats and small dogs. The keen coyote can trick an animal into becoming its dinner. Seeing or hearing an animal such as a bird or small deer nearby, the coyote pretends to be dead in order to attract the animal's attention. It lies down, unmoving, and waits for the nosy little creature to come in for a closer look. When it does—wham! The coyote has its meal.

The crafty coyote also uses other animal species to help it hunt for food. A coyote will sometimes follow herds of elk or bison. A lone coyote does not usually try to kill such large animals. Instead, it looks for smaller animals, such as rabbits and mice, that are stirred from their holes as the herds pass above them. Another favorite hunting trick of the coyote is to follow badgers. Badgers use their strong, tough claws to dig into the burrows of rabbits and ground squirrels. When a badger digs up a small rodent, a coyote may be lurking in the background. After letting the badger do the hard work of digging, the coyote then darts in and steals the prey.

Teamwork

When hunting with other coyotes, teamwork plays a large part in the success of a hunt. One coyote can wait at the end of an animal tunnel, such as a gopher hole, while another coyote digs at the entrance. When the animal runs away from the digging noise at one end, the other coyote grabs the prey in its powerful jaws.

This same kind of teamwork is useful when hunting larger animals such as deer, antelope, or elk.

Coyote Teamwork

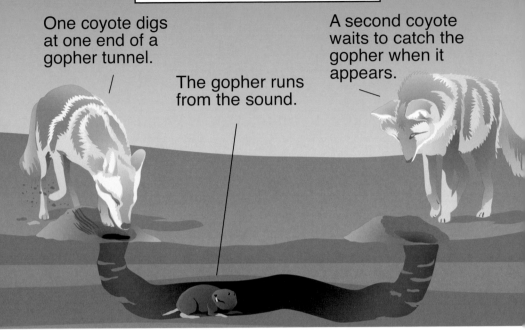

One coyote digs at one end of a gopher tunnel.

The gopher runs from the sound.

A second coyote waits to catch the gopher when it appears.

One coyote in a pack chases the prey until that coyote grows tired. At that point, another coyote picks up the chase. Coyotes will run this tag-team chase until the large animal is too tired to run any longer. When the coyotes sense the animal's weakness, they strike!

They circle the animal and begin to bite at its legs, sides, and rump, to tire it even more. The first coyote to move in for the kill is the alpha male. It lunges toward the animal and sinks its sharp, powerful teeth into the prey's throat. Its jaws clamp down hard on the creature's neck, and the pressure soon begins to cut off the animal's air.

Other members of the pack surround the animal. They use their claws to scratch at the animal's sides and rear. They also bite, tear, and slash with their teeth, but they are careful to stay out of the way of the animal's kicks. The alpha coyote tightens its grip on the prey by pressing down even harder on the animal's throat. The animal struggles, kicks, and bucks, but in minutes the alpha coyote's grip cuts off its oxygen. Out of air, the prey falls to the ground. The other pack members continue to dart in and out, quickly nipping and biting until the prey stops moving. The animal soon dies from the lack of air, from blood loss, or from shock. When the animal is no longer moving, the feeding begins.

CHAPTER THREE

Mealtime

Mealtime is a loud, excited, but organized affair in a coyote pack. Just as every coyote in the pack has a role to play during the hunt, each one does its part at mealtime. After each member has eaten, very little of the prey remains. Once the pack finishes with its prey, every member has benefited from the kill.

Feeding Time

Unlike other predators that eat in large groups such as wolves or even lions, coyotes are fairly calm during mealtime. Some yipping and snapping can occur between pack members, but scientists have observed little infighting among the pack at feeding time. Although different members of the pack eat different parts of the prey, every member shares in the feast when there is a large kill.

The coyotes work fast to eat as much of the kill as they can. Soon, the ground and every pack member are awash in the blood of the prey. While some coyotes eat, the rest of the pack circles the kill anxiously, barking, howling, and watching for other predators or scavengers. Those who are not ripping and tearing at the prey wait their turn, ready to alert the rest of the pack if danger is sighted.

All coyotes within the pack will defend the carcass against other coyotes or scavengers such as foxes or hawks. If scavengers or other predators attempt to steal the kill, all members go on high alert. They bark at and chase away any animal, including lone

Coyotes feed on a carcass. Coyotes in a pack take turns eating and watching for predators.

Coyotes rip apart an elk carcass. Coyotes eat quickly to avoid sharing their kill with other predators.

coyotes or coyotes from other packs. They leave their kill only if they have all eaten or if they are unsuccessful at scaring off larger predators such as bears or mountain lions.

An Orderly Affair

When it is time to feed, the alpha coyotes eat first. They rip open the animal's stomach with their sharp fangs and incisors, spilling the internal organs. They push away the stomach and intestines and start to feed on the animal's kidneys, liver, lungs, and fatty tissue. These are the richest parts of the animal, the parts filled with the most nutrients. Only after the soft internal organs have been eaten will they turn their attention to the tough muscles. When the alpha pair has had their fill, the other members take their turns at the carcass.

Using their pointed fangs, the beta members of the pack rip off chunks of the animal's flesh. Big, ragged hunks of muscle are torn away and swallowed quickly. Sinews are pulled and snapped away from the connecting muscles and swallowed whole. They use their molars to crack the prey's bones in order to suck out the rich marrow. The coyotes rip, tear, gnaw, suck, and swallow until they are full or until there is hardly anything edible left.

At the end of their feast, all that usually remains of the animal is its skin, its fur, the contents of its stomach, and large fragments of broken, gnawed bones. Sinews, muscles, and even cartilage have been totally stripped from the bones. The bones, especially the ribs, have chew marks from the coyotes' incisor teeth. In the winter, or when food is scarce, coyotes also eat the skin and fur of their prey. They devour the bones as well—all in the attempt to keep away hunger and survive the lean times.

Members of the pack stay at the kill site until they have finished with the carcass. Depending on the size of the animal and the number of coyotes within the pack, this may take hours or even days.

After the bones are picked clean, coyotes roll themselves in the remains of the carcass, mixing their scent with that of the dead animal. Scientists do not know exactly why they do this, but some think the coyotes leave their scent to mark the kill as a part of their territory. They also mark the site by urinating and leaving scat around the remains. Afterwards, with their coats covered in the drying blood of their kill, the coyotes either return to their den or find a place to hide and rest up for the next hunt.

Feeding the Pups

Mealtime is not over yet if pups are part of the pack. The alpha male or one or two associate coyotes take food from the kill site back to the pups and their mother at the den. The den is usually an old badger or fox hole that the alpha female has enlarged for use as a nursery for her pups. Only she and the alpha male are allowed to enter the den while the pups are being nursed. Because the pups are born blind and totally dependent on her, the alpha female will not leave them until they are about two months old. Therefore, she relies on the alpha male and the pack associates to provide her and her babies with food.

After getting a belly full of meat at the kill site, the alpha male or a beta member of the pack returns to the den and spits up a portion of its food. If the pups have begun to eat meat—usually around three

A coyote pup comes out of its den. Pups usually begin to eat meat at three or four weeks of age.

---

or four weeks of age—they eagerly eat the **regurgitated** food. The alpha female eats it as well. At times, however, her mate or an associate from the pack will bring her back chunks of meat from the kill site. If the pups are not old enough for solid food, pack members regurgitate only enough food for the nursing mother.

Whether working alone or with a pack, the coyote's intelligence and excellent scavenging, hunting, and killing techniques make it an exceptional predator. Its ability to adapt to almost any environment has allowed it to thrive even in the face of its enemies.

Surviving and Thriving

Native American legends describe the coyote as a trickster, an animal that always finds a way to survive. These legends reinforce the fact that the coyote is a wily survivor. It can eat discarded human food, trash, and dead animals. It can live in the driest conditions in southwestern deserts or the coldest Canadian forests. And, even when faced with threats in the wild and from humans, the coyote finds a way to not only survive, but thrive.

Few Natural Enemies

Adult coyotes do not have many natural enemies. Bears, wolves, and cougars sometimes kill adult coyotes, but the greatest threat from other animals is competition for food. Large predators such as wolves and cougars eat many of the same foods as coyotes, which sometimes makes it difficult for the coyotes

A cougar chases a coyote across the snow. Sometimes large animals like cougars kill coyotes.

to find food. The coyotes have, however, figured out a way around this. When sharing a habitat with animals such as cougars or a wolf pack, coyotes often resort to more scavenging. They follow the larger predators and wait until they have killed and eaten their meal. When those predators move on, the coyotes eat the leftovers. Coyotes do the same with bears, following them to their fishing spots and eating the remains of the fish the bears leave behind.

Threatened Pups

Coyote pups face another problem from large predators. Cougars and bears see them as a source of food. For this reason, coyotes keep their pups hidden in the den until they are several weeks old. The mother coyote stays with them at all times until they are about a month old. Only then will the pups be allowed to venture outside for short periods of time.

When the pups are allowed to explore the world outside the den, an adult is always close by. The adult keeps a close watch for predators, including wolves, bobcats, and even some birds. Large birds such as eagles and vultures have been known to swoop down and snatch young coyotes. If danger is sensed, the pups will be moved. The adult coyotes scout out and dig another den in a safer location. Then they carry the pups in their mouths to the new den. At times, a coyote pair or pack will use up to four dens before the pups are six months old.

When predators such as cougars, wolves, or eagles are near, the pack goes on the defensive. The alpha female and her pups hide in the den while the rest of the pack crowds around to defend the den and the pups. With his teeth bared, the alpha male takes the lead, yipping and growling at the unwelcome intruders. The associate coyotes help by growling and lunging at the predator if it comes too close to the den. Although their main purpose is to scare the intruder away, the pack will attack and even kill an animal they consider to be a threat.

Sometimes, however, the predator may be either too fast or too large for the coyotes to ward off. There may even be more than one intruder. At times like these, the only thing the coyotes can do is run away. If this is the course of action, the alpha female and her pups are in grave danger. Some pups may be lost. In fact, only about two pups in a litter of three to ten pups will survive their first eight months of life. Those that do not survive fall prey to other predators, to disease, or they die from dangers presented by humans.

Deadly Diseases

The coyote's other natural enemy is disease. Many coyotes in the wild die each year from diseases. Few make it past the age of six. They become infected through their prey or from stray dogs that have illnesses. One skin disease called mange causes a coyote to lose its fur. Without its fur to protect it, the coyote could easily die from the extreme heat or cold of its environment. Worms are parasites that weaken

Coyote pups explore outside their den. The coyote mother lets the pups outside once they are about a month old.

coyotes by sucking their blood and eating away at the tissues of the heart, liver, and other vital organs. Rabies and distemper also lead to deaths in coyotes. These two aggressive diseases are passed from animal to animal in the wild and can cause a very painful, sometimes prolonged death. Coyotes also suffer from diseases transmitted by mites, lice, and ticks. But, the most dangerous threat to the coyote is not a disease or another wild animal. The coyote's most dangerous enemy is humans.

Humans as a Threat

Humans have made it increasingly difficult for the coyote to survive. In the 1800s and 1900s, people killed coyotes in large numbers using poisons, traps, and guns. Although poisons and steel traps are no longer used, humans still make life difficult for the coyote.

As a result of early killing and poisoning methods, coyotes spread out to avoid contact with humans. But humans then expanded their territories. They destroyed thousands of acres of forests to build new cities and expanded existing cities into prairie and desert lands. To survive, the coyotes learned to adapt to these new city environments.

Each year four hundred thousand coyotes die as a result of human contact. Some are hit by cars on streets and highways. Some die when people put poison into pet food and leave it out for the coyotes to find and eat. Still others are killed when farmers

A coyote stands in the middle of a busy street. Thousands of coyotes are hit by cars every year.

leave poisoned sheep and goat carcasses for the coyotes to feed on. People sometimes do this when coyotes attack their livestock or injure their pets.

Government agencies kill thousands of coyotes each year in order to protect their prey. In 1996 alone, the Wildlife Services Department killed over eighty thousand coyotes. Fish and game organizations in

The Wildlife Services Department kills thousands of coyotes each year. This is done to keep coyote populations under control.

North America hold contests at various times of the year to see how many coyotes can be hunted within a given amount of time. The Wildlife Services Department kills coyotes by shooting them from helicopters, gassing their dens, digging them out of their dens and shooting them, and leaving poisoned food pellets for them to eat.

These legal killing methods are used to keep the coyote population under control. If left alone, coyotes could overpopulate an area and kill too many other animals. For example, in the Monomoy Wildlife Refuge in Massachusetts, the government has to kill some coyotes in order to protect the birds that live there.

Despite the dangers they face, many coyotes live in North America today. The coyote continues to flourish and thrive. Its varied diet and habitat and its physical and mental strengths have enabled it to expand its territory. The future looks bright for the coyote, one of nature's most perfect predators.

GLOSSARY

adapt: To change to fit a new situation or environment.

alpha: The lead or most dominant animal in a group.

carrion: Dead animals.

food chain: The order in which organisms eat and are eaten.

habitat: The natural environment of a species.

omnivores: Animals that eat meat, vegetables, and fruits.

predators: Animals that hunt and kill other animals.

regurgitated: Chewed, swallowed, partially digested, then vomited.

scat: Droppings.

scavenge: To feed on dead animals or garbage.

subspecies: A variety or kind of species.

FOR FURTHER EXPLORATION

Books

David Alderton, *Foxes, Wolves, and Wild Dogs of the World*. New York: Facts on File, 1994. Discusses the characteristics of the earth's wild canines.

Suzanne J. Murdico, *Animal Attacks: Coyote Attacks*. New York: Childrens Press, 2000. Explores the facts and reasons surrounding coyote attacks.

Phyllis J. Perry, *Crafty Canines: Coyotes, Foxes, and Wolves*. New York: Franklin Watts, 1999. Examines the tricks and adapting techniques of foxes, wolves, and coyotes.

Stephen R. Swinburne, *Coyote: North America's Dog*. Honesdale, PA: Boyds Mills Press, 1999. Distinguishes between the coyote and its cousin, the wolf.

Internet Source

Mike Finkel, "The Ultimate Survivor," *Audubon Magazine*. http://magazine.audubon.org.

Websites

Alien Explorer (www.alienexplorer.com). Explores the wonders of planet Earth and includes articles on wildlife and ecology.

Animal Protection Institute (www.api4animals. org). Website dedicated to educating the public about animals and human interaction with them.

Desert Foothills Land Trust (www.dflt.org). Filled with information on the Sonoran Desert in Arizona and the animals and plant life that make up that environment.

Desert USA (www.desertusa.com). Great site for researching America's desert habitats. Includes wildlife and tourism information.

Environmental News Network (www.enn.com). Website dedicated to news regarding the environment and conservation.

Wolf J. Lupus (www.wolfjlupus.com). Features articles, personal essays, and information on wild canines.

INDEX

PICTURE CREDITS

ABOUT THE AUTHOR

A native of Tarboro, North Carolina, Teresa L. Hyman is a professional editor and writer living in Overland Park, Kansas. She and her husband, Derrick, are the parents of two children, Briana and Devin. Hyman enjoys researching her Native American and African American ancestry and studying Native American and African American literature and art.